THE TRIP NOT TAKEN

For Ilene,

Enjoy!

Amy

The Trip Not Taken

Amy Ross

Paperback ISBN-13 978-0-578-85042-9

3 5 7 9 10 8 6 4 2

Thank you, dear friends, and a special
thanks to Uriah, Philip and Miles who,
I think, would not be too surprised.

Contents

It was May 22, 2020, and if not for COVID-19, I would have been enjoying a two-week tour through the Baltic capitals. Instead I was sitting in my living room, under statewide quarantine, worrying about the world, and dreaming of a tour that wasn't happening.

On that day, according to the tour itinerary, our group would have been staying at the Elizabete Hotel in Riga, Latvia. I would have been meeting new people, trying new foods, and learning about the rich cultural history of a part of the world unfamiliar to me. In short, I would have been traveling.

The tour would have begun four days earlier in Vilnius, Lithuania, with the fifteen-person group convening at the Radisson Blu Astorija. In the days that followed, we would have explored the old city and gotten to know each other. After Vilnius, we would have boarded a well-appointed tour bus for the trip from Vilnius to Riga, taking in a few lakes and castles along the way.

The following day we would have walked Riga's Old Town, admiring churches and cathedrals—including St.

Mary's Cathedral, which boasts a 6,789-pipe organ. We would have enjoyed other public buildings—including the imposing House of the Blackheads, which was built in the fourteenth century as a guild for unmarried merchants, shipowners, and foreigners; as well as the opera house, which is a venue for ballet and where Mikhail Baryshnikov began his career. We would have been very tired at the end of that day!

I began my written account in real time (for me), on May 22, our second day in Riga. Rather than let the quarantine ruin my trip, I would write about the journey as if I was actually on it.

Enjoy! (Or, as they say in Latvia, *Izbaudi!*)

Elizabete Hotel
Riga, Latvia

Riga is cool and cloudy today, which is fine by me.

In the morning, our tour group was driven to the Gauja National Park—a beautiful park with mountains, castles, and Gutmanis Cave, which has a healing reputation that, according to a local legend, was created by the unending tears of a faithless wife. The healing legend was established in the seventeenth century and has been questioned ever since. Gutmanis Cave is Latvia's oldest tourist attraction–visitors have been writing their names on the cave walls for centuries.

The cave is 62 feet deep, 39 feet wide, and 33 feet high. All fifteen of us dutifully peered in and made our wishes.

We returned to Riga for a free afternoon and I decided to have another look at the Central Market (Centraltirgus), which occupies five former German zeppelin hangars. The interiors are designed in neoclassical and art deco styles. It's been operating as a community market since 1930.

I fell in love with open markets as a child when my family visited the Pike Place Market in Seattle. Today, while wandering through Centraltirgus, I purchased a selection of pastries to take back to my hotel room. They brightened it up like flowers.

The Zemenu Ragi (Strawberry Horns) was rich and creamy with vanilla filling squishing between the layers. The cookies were crisp and ginger-spiced.

Then I walked across town to the Riga Art Nouveau Museum.

The collection and the buildings around the museum are wonderful. As you may know, I'm fond of museum shops. This one, however, only sold teaspoons, thimbles and Victorian-style postcards. I'm finding that former Soviet countries have wonderful community markets and museums, but the museum gift shops are less developed. Unlike the sparkling glass cases one finds at MoMA and the Louvre, many former Soviet gift shops are modestly stocked. Capitalism has yet to bite that deeply, I suppose.

Tomorrow we leave for Tallinn!

Blu Sky Hotel
Tallinn, Estonia

The trip to Tallinn took about five hours because along the way we stopped at Parnu, an Estonian seaside resort once favored by the czars.

When the clouds cleared, the Gulf of Finland was beautiful.

With the stop in Parnu, we reached Tallinn at about 7 p.m. We're staying at the Blu Sky Hotel. Like the Elizabete in Riga, the Blu Sky is more modern than places I would choose on my own—but that also means our stay is pleasantly predictable.

The tour group dined in the rooftop bar. The view was fantastic.

Over dinner and drinks, we previewed tomorrow's itinerary. There would be ruins and museums and two meals-on-our own, lunch and dinner. As it grew later, my companions trailed away their rooms, but I stayed a bit longer, enjoying the view and anticipating the coming day. Where would I dine?

Tallinn, Estonia

After breakfast at the hotel, we visited the ruins of St. Birgit's Convent, a short distance from the Old Town. A fourteenth-century monastery for both monks and nuns, St. Birgit's was among the largest convents in northern Europe until 1577, when Ivan the Terrible sacked and burnt it.

As you can see in the picture, it's most definitely ruined now.

After wandering through the grounds at St. Birgit's,

we returned to Tallinn for lunch and dinner on our own. I'd heard of a crepe restaurant called Kompressor. It describes itself as legendary, and I couldn't resist.

I ordered a smoked salmon and cheese crepe, and one with blueberries for dessert, finishing with an espresso. Delicious. I enjoyed sitting with others at the large communal table. I'm finding that Estonians (in Tallinn, at least) are quite comfortable speaking English, which is great because my Estonian is limited to short, polite phrases, like "hello," "please," "thank you," and "goodbye" (*tere, palun, aitäh,* and *hüvasti*).

The rest of the afternoon I spent meandering through the Kumu Art Museum. Both the museum and its gift shop are less old-fashioned than Riga's Art Nouveau museum.

I liked Kumu better, and yet not as much, as the Art Nouveau museum. While the Kumu's modernity was refreshing, I miss the homey interiors of the Riga museum.

I enjoyed the Estonian art I saw, and there was an exhibit about the 1937 World's Fair in Paris and the pavilion sponsored by Lithuania, Latvia, and Estonia. The World Fair's architectural rules required that pavilion exteriors be modern in design, as neutral as possible, and without any nationalist features. In an editorial comment, the exhibition curator noted that perhaps the Baltic countries succeeded only too well in their neutral design.

I learned that the Baltics brought home numerous grand prizes; honorary diplomas; and gold, silver, and bronze medals. It was also noted by the curator that several countries had earned laurels for designs that were quite nationalistic, barely following the architectural rules at all.

The Kumu's atrium provided lots of opportunities for people-watching, and then I walked back through the old city. I love medieval architecture—low buildings leaning into twisting cobblestone streets. It feels very cozy.

For dinner, I chose Restoran Farm along the old city wall.

Inside the restaurant, rich pelts decorated the dark walls, and a most remarkable taxidermic tableau of wolf and boar, raucously dining, occupied the window. The beasts were seated like humans at a rustic wooden table full of empty plates and glasses, their heads thrown back in laughter as though regaling each other with off-color jokes. Beside their table a graceful fox was easing past, walking on hind legs, wearing a flowered hat, and carrying a chic handbag. A shy rabbit hovered to one side, like an uncertain waiter. It reminded me of a Weimar fairy tale.

For dinner, I had an excellent entrée of veggies and beef, served with slices of richly buttered black bread.

After dinner, I walked back to the hotel, taking my time, walking down intriguing side streets. It felt impossible to get lost.

I'm writing this in the hotel bar. It's almost 10 p.m. and the sun is just dipping toward the horizon.

Tonight, I'm trying Vana Tallinn, one of Estonia's most popular drinks. It's a tasty concoction of Jamaican rum, hand-made vanilla and cinnamon extracts, and natural citrus oils. It's as delicious as it sounds. According to the advertisement placed on the bar, Estonia sells more than two million bottles annually, in twenty-seven countries.

In the morning we're going into the countryside, where I suppose there actually could be wolves, boar, and foxes—although none holding wine glasses or carrying stylish handbags. Seeing a shy rabbit is more likely.

Tallinn, Estonia

We spent much of yesterday in rural Estonia at Rocca-al-Mare, an open-air museum about five miles east of Tallinn along the Gulf of Finland. It's a reproduction of an eighteenth-century rural fishing village, and spans more than 175 acres, with eighty buildings. It felt like a happy memory of the good old days.

We returned to Tallinn after lunch, and along with about half the tour group I went for a walk along the medieval wall and saw the flower vendors at the Viru Gate.

My traveling companions are pleasant and there's never an obligation for all of us to go to the same place. Lisa, the tour director, is easygoing unless we're on the bus—then she makes sure no one is left behind, which I appreciate. At the Rundale Palace, on our way to Riga, I was the last one on board. The Palace has 138 rooms and I'd gotten turned around. I was greatly relieved to see the bus still waiting and Lisa impatiently tapping her foot.

Tonight's dinner is on our own. I walked to Grenka, a casual seafood restaurant serving fish harvested from the North Sea. I ordered seafood soup, which was very tasty. I thought it might be like a bouillabaisse, but the herbs and spices were quite different. The flavors were darker, less suggestive of sunny southern Europe.

It was a good day.

Grand Hotel Europe
St. Petersburg, Russia

We left Tallinn for St. Petersburg early and spent a long day on the bus. Our itinerary took us from Tallinn, along the Gulf of Finland, across the Russian border, and on to St. Petersburg. The trip lasted about eight hours. The trips between Vilnius, Riga, and Tallinn were each only half as long.

The day was sunny and along the way we stopped at Narva to eat our box lunches. Narva is a military port city on the Gulf of Finland. With today's sunshine, even the heavy, gray fortifications seemed less ominous than they were built to be.

A few more hours brought us to the border between Estonia and Russia. The locked gates of the customs station blocked both sides of the road and our bus pulled into a long line of cars and trucks waiting to be searched.

Even when I was reading about this trip in the familiarity of my American living room, I was uneasy about this border crossing. I'm a Cold-War kid and most of my information on unfriendly border crossings comes from a movie—*The Spy Who Came in From the Cold* (especially the part set in Berlin). Richard Burton was a fine actor and he communicated an overpowering sense of danger.

Russian Customs is very serious and very official—like most. The officers were heavily armed and scowling. They did have an attractive sniffer dog with them, who had melting brown eyes and might have liked ear scritches, but I didn't push it.

After a close baggage inspection by the cheerless guards, and a good going-over by the sniffer dog, we were ready—our visas checked, our passports stamped. The bus was back on its way. We drove onto a busy freeway, which took us into St. Petersburg. The freeway seemed like any of the freeways leading into any of the big Western cities I've visited. It was a little disappointing that we approached this beautiful city, so rich in history, on a road that felt so average.

But our hotel, the Grand Hotel Europe, turned that around. It was old and palatial and glamorous. This was more like it! There was a grand staircase of white marble, and golden chandeliers that caught the light.

The rooms are comfortable and well appointed.

After the group dinner, I set out on a short walk, just around the block, as I always do in a new city.

The hotel has a nice little outdoor café. I took a table and ordered a glass of wine, and enjoyed the fresh evening air. In this part of the world and at this time of year, the sun doesn't stay set for long. Days ease into warm twilights until the sun, which had barely disappeared behind the horizon, slowly rises again.

I think I'm going to enjoy this city very much.

St. Petersburg, Russia

Привет! (This means *hello* and sounds to me like "Privyet")

This was our first day navigating a Russian-speaking world and I think we're all glad to be with a guide. At the hotel, everyone speaks charmingly accented English, but once we stepped out the front doors, it couldn't be depended on. I can be generally polite in several languages, however, I found Russian especially difficult, partly because of the unfamiliar Cyrillic alphabet.

А Б В Г Д Е Ё Ж З
И Й К Л М Н О П
Р С Т У Ф Х Ц Ч
Ш Щ Ъ Ы Ь Э Ю Я

I didn't have much oomph today, but it worked out. We spent much of the day walking easily between nearby sights, starting in Palace Square.

Palace Square is a huge parade ground bordered by the Winter Place (now the main building of the Hermitage), the General Staff Building and the Admiralty, with the Alexander Column in the center. The neoclassical architecture inspires the heart and commands the eye—as it's meant to.

Then we went to Nevsky Prospekt, the historic shopping district. The streets are lined with a dazzling selection of department stores, boutiques, and bookstores—many in beautiful neoclassical buildings. The lack of the usual big, western vendors was absolutely refreshing.

But I was tired and the Nevsky Prospekt was quite busy, so when I saw the Soviet Café, I dove in.

It was interesting and unexpected. I ordered an espresso and read the description offered in four languages.

The café is an artful reconstruction of a Soviet *kvartira*—Russian for a flat or apartment. It's stuffed with items that each Soviet family had: a carpet on the wall, a gramophone, and a huge cupboard with porcelain and glass. It felt grandmotherly.

On my way out, I took a matchbook to prove I'd been there and rejoined the crowded Nevsky.

In a few blocks I came to the Singer House. It was built by the Russian branch of the Singer Sewing Machine Company and was completed in 1914, just a few years before the start of the Russian Revolution. At the time it was considered very up-to-date, with air conditioning, elevators, and modern materials. The architecture is nuanced. The six-story art nouveau building is crowned with a glass tower, which in turn is topped by a glass globe, creating the impression of a substantial elevation, yet subtle enough not to overshadow nearby churches and cathedrals.

The building houses Dom Knigi—*House of Books*—St. Petersburg's huge, beautiful bookstore. Inside I found a gorgeous marble staircase, stylish Venetian and art nouveau decorations, and a great many books.

They also have a tantalizing selection of postcards. I bought several.

The Singer Café was one floor up from the bookstore. I found a table by an arched window and had tea and cherry pirozhki while I waited to meet the group for the curator-led tour of the Hermitage, which was to follow shopping on Nevsky Prospekt.

I had been told by several people to expect Russians to be dour and unsmiling. But I should have known that was just a stereotype. The Russians I've gotten to know will smile if I say something amusing—even if they wouldn't necessarily have done so upon first meeting. It's not one of their social conventions. When traveling, I probably smile too much, making too much eye contact with strangers (after all, everyone is one). But here, I've been resisting that. Most of the time I try for a rueful look, burdened with little hope.

Lisa got us to the Hermitage in time for the curated

tour. Walking in, I was dazzled by how palatial it is. From 1732–1917, it was the winter palace and the official residence of Russian czars.

Now it is an internationally heralded museum of art and culture. The Hermitage occupies six other historic buildings, and the collection would take years, perhaps a lifetime, to see properly. The guided tour just skimmed the surface, but provided the perfect orientation for when I go back on my own in a few days.

Last winter, when I was considering various tours, the Hermitage was my goal, and I decided to stay two extra days so I could spend more time wandering its galleries.

After the museum tour, the bus returned us to the hotel. I was very glad to relax in my room until it was time for a light dinner in the hotel's Mezzanine Cafe.

St. Petersburg, Russia

доброе утро! (This means *good morning* and sounds to me like "dobroye utro"—a sweet-sounding phrase, soft on the ear.)

After breakfast, we drove to the Peterhof, another of the czars' extra palaces. This one is about twenty miles from St. Petersburg, back toward Estonia. The road we took follows the waterfront and was very picturesque. It was sunny and warm, but not yet humid, as it's likely to be later in the summer.

After the Hermitage, I was a bit blasé towards over-the-top ornamentation, which aptly describes the Peterhof. There's only so such gold and marble and architectural fabulousness one can absorb. I didn't spend long inside. For me, the best features were the fountains and Olga's Pavilion.

The Grand Duchess Olga was Nicholas I's daughter. In 1846, Nicholas built a home for Olga and her new husband, Prince Karl of Würtenburg, on the Peterhof grounds. It was designed in the style of the country villas of Sicily. After all, the union had been decided in Palermo.

We were on our own for lunch, so a few of us walked to the Linea Restaurant. The menu was in Russian, but with pictures, which helped. Plus, Lisa had made suggestions.

After lunch we returned to the Grand Hotel and I toddled around the corner to Beluga, a crazily expensive store I'd noticed on a previous walk. They specialize in amber and fur. I guiltily ran my fingers through the rich, thick furs, but it was the amber jewelry that really took my breath away.

My Russian fairy godmother must have been watching because I left unscathed. Must. Not. Return.

I wanted to see the Peter and Paul Fortress, which holds the Peter and Paul Cathedral, and this free afternoon seemed right. I hurried over to clear my head, which I had nearly lost at Beluga.

Peter the Great built both the fortress and cathedral in the eighteenth century as a defense against invading forces. They are considered the first and oldest landmarks in St. Petersburg. I'm tempted to compare the fortress to Latvia's oldest landmark: an autographed wishing cave. For many years the Peter and Paul Fortress served as a prison for political prisoners.

This evening, we went to dinner at Literaturnoye Kafé, an historic restaurant that was a favorite of eighteenth-century writers, poets, and journalists.

Pushkin is said to have eaten his last meal here. I hope he had the mushroom soup—it was delicious!

Tomorrow, half the tour group flies home. The rest of us are staying two extra days. I'm nervous about being here without a tour guide, but it will be okay. I won't be alone—several people I like on the tour are staying, too. My friends are those who take life at a relaxed pace—even when touring. It's fun to stop at bars and restaurants along the way.

First, I'll go back to the Hermitage, and then visit the Church of Our Savior on Spilled Blood.

до завтра—until tomorrow.

St. Petersburg, Russia

всем привет! (This means *hello there*, and sounds to me like "sem-privyet.")

Today was the first of my two days in St. Petersburg without a guide (though I'm still officially on the tour). Since it was the Hermitage that drew me here, that was my first destination.

All the excessive descriptions of the Hermitage's architecture are absolutely accurate. It is huge, luxurious in the extreme, and has the largest collection of paintings in Europe.

I had admired the opulence when we were here on our first day in St. Petersburg, so I went directly to the European modernism galleries where I found myself surrounded by the paintings of my favorite artists: Matisse, Picasso, Derain, Dufy. It was heaven. The Matisses especially grabbed my attention.

After about two hours of roaming through expressionist and impressionist galleries, I was ready for lunch and went to the museum's café. The food there was unadorned Russian and delicious. Somehow I didn't expect authentic borscht to be my favorite.

Then it was straight back to the galleries.

However, much as I love museums, after a few more hours I needed fresh air and a rest. I wandered through the expanse of the Hermitage, searching for an exit, and finally found one in a gallery of banners, standards, and flags, which is dedicated to all things military.

The walk back to the hotel took me to the Church of the Savior on Spilled Blood. The church, completed in 1907, is formerly Russian Orthodox and situated along the Griboyedov channel embankment.

The church was erected on the site where political nihilists assassinated Emperor Alexander II in March 1881. The church was funded by the Romanov imperial family in honor of Alexander II, and the suffix "on [Spilled] Blood" refers to his assassination.

Now it's a secular museum known for its art nouveau mosaics. It's glorious—everything so rich and colorful, with glowing mosaics everywhere.

It was hard to leave the mosaics, but the Hermitage had sapped my only-human strength. Reaching the hotel, I rested in my room until it was time to meet friends for dinner. We walked to a nearby restaurant.

They serve Japanese, Northern European and Uzbek cuisines. I liked it very much, but the borscht was better at the Hermitage. (I've waited years to say something like that!)

Tomorrow is my last day in St. Petersburg and it will be even busier than today.

Спокойной ночи! (This means *good night*, and sounds to me like "spa-conyay-notche.")

St. Petersburg, Russia

мой последний день в России. (This means *this is my last day in Russia*, but I find it too complicated to sound out.)

The hotel breakfasts are wonderful. Sauerkraut, which until now I didn't know as a morning treat, is stored in the drum.

My friend, Sandra Freels, Professor Emerita of Russian at PSU, suggested many places to go in St. Petersburg. There are two I haven't done yet: to walk on both sides of the Neva from the Hermitage to the Blagoveshchenskiy Bridge, and to visit the Russian State Museum. I'll do both today.

Walking riverside and along the canals, I was reminded of walking beside the Seine.

St. Petersburg is one of a group of seven cities often called "The Venice of the North"; it shares this name with Amsterdam, Bruges, Copenhagen, Hamburg, Manchester and Stockholm. Like Venice, all these northern European cities have a network of canals.

On the way to the Russian State Museum, I stopped at a touristy spot called the Museum of Vodka. What fun! I had no idea Russian vodka had so many variations.

From there it was just a short walk to the Russian State Museum. I managed to avoid, again, the ruinously expensive amber at Beluga. I mustn't even think of the beautiful necklaces and earrings they sell there.

The Russian State Museum, like the Hermitage, is comprised of several palaces. Unlike the Hermitage, the focus is on Russian rather than Western art.

I concentrated on the icons. More than 6000 are displayed there.

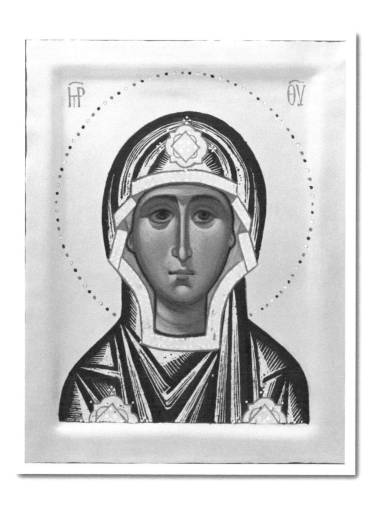

From there I hurried to the Hotel Astoria (in Russian that would be отель астория) to meet two friends from the tour, Janice and Gloria. The Astoria is a sumptuous shack across from St. Isaac's Square and not far from the Nevsky. It's amusing that the Astors of New York—after whom Astoria, Oregon was named—were here, too, as well as in Lithuania. I suppose it all comes down to the fur trade.

We dined and strolled back to the Grand.

After these wonderful days in St Petersburg, I have a change of plans to announce: I'm not coming home right away.

For the past few days I've been rethinking my original plan to return to Portland tomorrow. Each day it appeals less. I imagine myself leaving this elegant hotel very early tomorrow morning and after twenty hours of grueling air travel finding myself worn to a frazzle and back on Whitaker Street, the adventure over all too soon. So I won't leave tomorrow. I canceled my tickets and will spend the summer in Tallinn.

I'm already in the Baltics. Why not make the most of it?

Tomorrow I'm moving to the Hotel Astoria and will be in touch. And I'm going to stop counting the days. That was a tour habit. Time will just flow now.

Ma tean, et see saab olema lõbus! (I know it will be fun! in Estonian)

отель астория
(Hotel Astoria)
St. Petersburg, Russia

Several days have passed and I'm still at the Hotel Astoria, finalizing plans for June and July. It's lovely place to linger and is near the Singer House in case I run low on pirozhki.

This hotel is also only a block or so from St. Isaac's Square and the late- eighteenth century heroic statue, the Bronze Horseman. The horseman is Peter the Great (of course). Catherine the Great commissioned it in 1782.

Not far away is St. Isaac's Cathedral. Originally Russian Orthodox, it was dedicated to Saint Isaac of Dalmatia, patron saint of Peter the Great, who was born on the saint's feast day in 1672. It became a state museum in 1931.

Another beautiful Russian Orthodox interior.

Regarding Tallinn, I've been looking online for an Airbnb apartment and found something unique. It's called Rapunzel's Tower—the name is perfect! With high windows, the tower is more than six centuries old. It used to be part of the city wall. Now it's a rental for tourists.

However, it isn't available until July, so I've decided to return to Riga for the rest of June. I rented an apartment there and will settle into my romantic tower in July.

A week ago, as I waved goodbye to the remaining members of the tour group, I started to feel anxious and thought, *This is crazy! What have I done? I must leave with them!* It was beginning to sink in, I was on my own in Mother Russia. How could I possibly get across the border without a tour guide? Those frightening Cold War images rose in my mind again.

I didn't sleep well that night. Fortunately, before the tour guide left, she introduced us to Svetlana, a friend of hers who lives here. In the morning, I rang Svetlana and we met at the Singer Cafe.

Svetlana is a well-traveled woman and talking with her turned my mood around. What had seemed ill advised if not impossible began to feel within my reach again. I stopped fretting and made airline reservations for Riga.

After that, I spent several days revisiting the Hermitage and the Russian State Museum, and wandering along the Neva. Then came the afternoon when I boldly returned to Beluga for amber.

More to come once I'm settled in Riga.

Riga, Latvia

Sveiki draugi! (Hello friends in Latvian.)

I'm glad to be back in Riga. I like it here. Admittedly, I've only seen the Old Town so far, but the city has a good vibe.

I try to speak Latvian as much as possible, but rely heavily on Google Translate for anything beyond basic pleasantries. I did learn to say, "Sorry about Trump." That phrase gets a lot of use and sounds like "kayl par Trump." When I say it, I shake my head sadly, adding, "Es nekad par vinu nebalsoju." *I didn't vote for him.*

My Airbnb apartment is near St. Peter's Church, a well-known spot.

The Church borders Riga's main square where the annual Christmas market is held. The large red buildings are the House of the Blackheads; originally erected during the first third of the fourteenth century for the Brotherhood of Blackheads, a guild for unmarried merchants, ship owners, and foreigners.

The apartment is small, but light and airy. The living room window looks into trees and across the street to the Mentzendorff House, a mansion built in the seventeenth century by the successful Mentzendorff merchant family. They made a great deal of money and now their family home is a museum.

I visited the museum soon after moving into my apartment. The guide walked us through many rooms. There are fully restored wall and ceiling paintings, a 17th-century kitchen with a chimneypiece, the children's room, as well as the cellars and attic. The guide was very thorough.

There are exhibition spaces for glass-blowing demonstrations and tile painting, and the house has rooms dedicated to poetry readings and concerts. It is wonderful to see so much happening in this historical building.

To live less like a tourist, I needed to find a grocery store. I hoped to shop where the locals do, and happily found that many do their shopping—grocery and otherwise—at the Centraltirgus (the Central Market), which I visited when here on the tour. Best of all, it's not far from my apartment.

When I want a change from the delicious but dense black bread so popular here, I pick up a bagette-style loaf from Anna at her bakery counter.

I wandered through the zeppelin hangars again, and brought home cold cuts, bread ... and breakfast pastries, of course.

On my second day here, I signed up for various tours. The first, my favorite, was Lunch in the Market. It was a two-hour tour of the food stalls. We went from vendor to vendor, trying Latvian favorites. I only saw (and tasted) a sliver of what was there.

My second-favorite was a boat tour on the canal that circled the Old Town.

We boarded at the Freedom Monument, which was completed in 1935. The statue sits along the canal, making the small boarding pier easy to find. After an hour on the canal, I confirmed without a doubt that Latvian and American ducks speak exactly the same language. It was a beautiful trip, slowly sailing from one side of Old Town and back again.

The third get-to-know-Riga-better tour focused on Old Town as a whole and took us through a gate in the city wall to a hip, artsy neighborhood called Miera Iiela ("Iiela" means *street*).

It was busy with Latvian hipsters, an adorable subset. The businesses here are less mainstream—they sell avant-garde art and unusual clothing. And there are numerous cafés selling fabulous coffee.

The tours did the trick. Now I'm exploring confidently on my own. I wander down intriguing little streets and I can always find my way home by triangulating on the spire on St Peter's.

St. Peter's (in Latvian: *Svētā Pētera Evaņģēliski luteriskā baznīca*) is a Lutheran church dedicated to St. Peter. The first mention of the St. Peter's Church is in records dating to 1209.

The original church was of masonry construction and it was left undamaged by a city fire in Riga that same year. There were second and third periods of construction in the 15th and 17th centuries. Then the reconstructions began.

It's a wonderful beacon home.

Riga, Latvia

Since arriving in Riga, I've been looking for a restaurant or cafe where I can be a regular. For me, that's an essential connection. After a few days, I found one: Muusu. That means *muse* in Latvian.

The vibe reminds me of West Café, my favorite restaurant in Portland. The bartender is friendly and handsome and the menu is excellent. Muusu's chef blends traditional Latvian dishes with western culinary trends. I often go there in the evening, sit at an outside table with a glass of wine and watch the twilight deepen. I'm even getting to know the owners, which makes me feel especially welcome. And it's only a short walk from my apartment. I can easily have a second glass of wine without worrying about stumbling on the cobblestones on my way home.

With that settled, I'm going further afield. The architecture in the art-nouveau district is so impressive.

I enjoy the unique and beautiful architecture, but sometimes it feels foreboding and otherworldly.

I was glad to get back to gentle Muusu for a quiet dinner on the patio.

Some exciting news—I have company! Amanda's avatar came over from Paris to see what Riga has to offer.

We'll wander the Central Market, drink coffee, and watch the day unfold. The plūmju pīrāgs (plum tart) at Bezē is delicious.

There's a Latvian phrase I particularly like: "Labi visiem." It means *nicely for everyone*. That's how Riga feels.

Riga, Latvia

After a delightful week, Amanda returned to Paris and tomorrow I leave for Tallinn. Yes, it's "ardievu, Riga" (*goodbye, Riga* in Latvian) and "tere, Tallinn" (*hello, Tallinn* in Estonian). I've had a wonderful time here and hate to go, but the tower apartment is almost ready.

To get to Tallinn, I'm using an intercity car service. For just 46 euros, they're sending an English-speaking driver to pick me up at the Riga apartment and four hours later, snap crackle pop, I'll be at Three Sisters, a boutique hotel in Tallinn. By staying there for the first two nights, I'll have time to scope out the neighborhood before accepting the keys to the tower.

Before leaving Riga, I've been revisiting my favorite haunts. I made last trips to the Central Market, to Muusu, and to the Black Magic Apothecary Bar, a grotto-like establishment where the cocktails and chocolate desserts are so good that I made two last trips.

I also took the canal tour again, but on a full round trip this time. We went out on the Dzelzcela River, where there are real ships and a bit more chop. That was unnerving.

On the farther shore, the new Latvian National Library reflected the sun. The library building, also called the Castle of Light, is very modern inside and out—but too much so for my tastes.

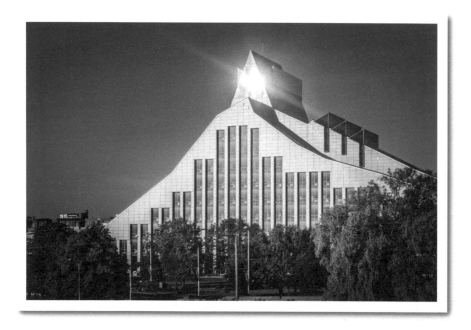

Until Tallinn, then. Some travelers say Tallinn's old city, although smaller, is the best of the three Baltic capitals.

Tik ilgi pagaidam (Latvian for "So long, for now").

Hattorpe Torn
Tallinn, Estonia

Tere, Mulle meeldib Tallinn siiani kõige paremin.

That's Estonian for "Hello, and I like Tallinn the best so far." Maybe the rumor about the Baltic capitals is true, however, Vilnius certainly deserves anther visit.

I'm acclimating very quickly. It helps that the hotel and tower are less than a block apart.

In Tallinn, the tower is known as Hattorpe Torn, but online it's Rapunzel's Tower. The tower is part of the old city's protective walls. The walls no longer completely surround the old city—only in sections, and my tower is in one of them. I love living here—the high ceilings, arched windows, and hardwood floors. It's a step back in time and I wake up to it every day.

To establish the essential restaurant connection in Tallinn, I've gone back to Farm (the place with the kooky tableau of wolf, boar, and fox), which isn't far from my tower. I've also gotten to know Sophija (left) and Marta who work in a nearby bakery and we meet occasionally after their shifts. As it was in Riga, the people of Tallinn are very friendly. They make me feel welcome.

Grocery shopping in Tallinn isn't quite as much fun as it was in Riga, there are no zeppelin hangers filled with delicious food and intriguing shops, but I have found Juustukuningad, a wonderful cheese shop. Bread, cheese and a hard-boiled egg make a nice lunch, especially with a glass of white wine. So far, I like their Sõir best. It's a soft cheese made with whole milk, cottage cheese, butter, eggs, salt, and flavored with caraway seeds. Dreamy.

There are so many restaurants and coffee shops that it seems there is a new one for every day. I particularly like Maiasmokk.

It was built in 1864 and is the oldest café continuously operating in Estonia. It has a welcoming German-Austrian vibe and a wonderful bakery. There is also a marzipan museum within the café.

Another favorite is Must Puudel (Black Poodle). It's more casual, with small outdoor tables on a lovely patio.

With so much to see—I haven't walked outside the city walls or taken the ferry to Helsinki or revisited Vilnius—I'm considering staying until Christmas. The tower's next renters aren't expected until January (they ski) and the photos I've seen of snowy Tallinn are absolutely charming—which, in a place this deeply cute, is really saying something.

Imagine Tallinn's Christmas market—the glowing lights, the snow, and the colorful holiday trinkets.

How can I leave without seeing that? And by Christmas maybe, just maybe, I'll be more at ease in at least one of these beautiful, difficult languages. In the meantime, here is my goodbye in all four: Su meilė (Lithuanian), Ar mīlestība (Latvian), Armastusega (Estonian), and С любовью (Russian).

And in English:
With love,

Amy

The Trip Not Taken is available online through Barnes and Noble and Amazon.

CPSIA information can be obtained
at www.ICGtesting.com
Printed in the USA
BVHW021723250721
612464BV00001B/1